GENTLY GRIEVING

*Taking Care of Yourself
by Telling Your Story*

Constance M. Mucha

D0064179

Paulist Press
New York/Mahwah, N.J.

Excerpts from Tom Golden's *Swallowed by a Snake: The Gift of the Masculine Side of Healing,* 2nd edition, 1996, 2000, Golden Healing Publishing LLC, Gaithersburg, MD. web<webhealing.com> are used with permission of the author.

Lines 10–24 of "Morning, Sacrament of Hope" (pp. 64 and 65) from *Seasons of Your Heart: Prayers and Reflections* by Macrina Wiederkehr, copyright © 1991. Reprinted by permission of HarperCollins Publishers, Inc.

Cover design by Cynthia Dunne

Library of Congress Cataloging-in-Publication Data

Mucha, Constance M.
    Gently grieving : taking care of yourself by telling your story / Constance M. Mucha.
        p. cm.—(IlluminationBooks)
    Includes bibliographcial references.
    ISBN 0-8091-4387-9 (alk. paper)
    1. Bereavement—Religious aspects—Christianity. 2. Grief—Religious aspects—Christianity. 3. Consolation. I. Title. II. Series.
        BV4905.3.M83 2006
        248.8'66—dc22

                                                          2005028976

Published by Paulist Press
997 Macarthur Boulevard
Mahwah, New Jersey 07430

www.paulistpress.com

Printed and bound in the United States of America

Contents

DEDICATION

In loving memory of my parents, Mary and Donald Dougherty, my brother, Donnie, who died too young, my sister Monica, my oldest son Francis who was stillborn, my second husband Doug and my good friend and professional colleague Betty. I have learned through the pain of these losses to be gentler with myself in the midst of my own deep sadness and while ministering to others as their pastoral counselor.

And to the many clients who have shared their stories with me as we became co-pilgrims on their journeys of pain. They learned to trust the process as they moved from mourning to morning.

Acknowledgments

I would like to thank Dr. Robert Wicks for the opportunity to write a book that could be a help to grieving people. Thanks, also, to Loyola Pastoral Counseling Department, which helped with my education as a pastoral counselor through the Masters, CAS and doctoral programs, and to Drs. Robert Davenport and Beverly Eanes, my mentors in grief therapy.

I would like to acknowledge Mother Catherine Grace and the All Saints Sisters of the Poor who helped to prepare me for my work in hospice through the Ministry at The Joseph Richey Hospice. They were a constant inspiration to my pioneer spirit.

Thanks to my husband, Joe, who is a daily inspiration to me. He gave up some of our precious moments together so that I could spend time on the book. His sense of humor and courage through his own loss experiences have touched my heart. He is a man of great strength and spirit.

Thanks also to my children: Colleen, Brian, Patrick, and Michael. They have traveled the mourning journey with me. Thanks also to my step-daughter Jean who is no stranger to grief. My children have been my best supports whenever I am engaged in any special project. They listen, encourage, and cheer me on.

My grandchildren and step-grandchildren insist that I take time to relax and have fun. Thank you: Zacchary, Ezekiel, Naomi, Sonja, Noelle, Austin, Aidan, Shelby, Sophia, Caitlin, and Chelsea.

I want to thank Virginia Kline for the typing and invaluable suggestions to the manuscript. Ginny has a way of gently nudging me to get going when I start to procrastinate.

Many thanks to Linda for sharing her story, and to my clients who, with tears and laughter, shared their stories.

Finally, thanks to my friends and additional support systems: my high school buddies, Pat Boyett, Nancy Francis, and finally, my friend and professional colleague, Peggy Greene. They can sense when to be quietly present and when to encourage me to move on. They have provided ongoing support during my deep sadness and listened to the retelling of my story many times.

Introduction

This book is "borne" out of my personal and professional experiences in losing loved ones and in facilitating the pain-filled work of clients. I have worked as a pastoral counselor for nineteen years and I continue to learn from the bereaved who touch my life in new ways as each one's story unfolds. When Dr. Robert Wicks asked me to write a book about helping people with the grief process, I wondered just what I could say that would be most useful to suffering people. I've read, studied, learned about and lived the heartbreak of loss. I've developed bereavement programs, led seminars, and started a bereavement center. I'm always in search of the best *way to help. Through all my experience, the common healing thread has been the telling and retelling of "The Story."*

"The Story" has formed history. It is the narration of events that informs, clarifies, and/or amuses the listener. Jesus used stories, such as the parable of the mustard seed, to teach his disciples (Matt 13:31–32, New Revised Standard Edition). Parents use stories to teach their children about faith, values, and derive lessons through experiences and family histories. Teachers in school often use stories to help clarify a lesson. As you think back about teachers you had along the way, how many classes do you remember as more engaging and realize that the lesson stayed with you because your teacher told a story that added interest and clarity to the lesson. The story can be told as fact or fiction, in prose, poetry, or song. In grief, your story is your remaining connection to your lost loved one. As the storyteller, you will be telling about your experiences, which will bring tears and laughter to your listeners. These anecdotes will define your life and death experiences with the deceased, now one of your ancestors. Your story will be a significant part of your family history to pass on to future generations.

The grief process is the experience of restoring and maintaining the balance of your physical, emotional, psychological, and spiritual health. Keep in mind, the primary teacher that will help you understand the process is *you*, and the lessons learned will come from your own story. As you tell and retell your story, you will begin to understand it as a key component of your healing process.

The topic of grief is very broad. The focus of this book will be dealing with the death of a loved one and some of the secondary losses that may follow. I will describe the process and some effective coping strategies that I have found useful in helping people heal. Even though each story is unique, as you read the stories and discussions that follow, consider how these accounts apply to your own personal experience. The themes of tears and laughter should strike a familiar chord with you. Each chapter has been written to describe a different aspect of the grieving process, and you may find some chapters apply more to your personal story than others. This book can also serve as a reference guide when you need help or clarification on one aspect of your grief.

We know that life is never the same after the death of a loved one. *Gently Grieving* begins with the first mourning of deep sadness and takes you to the dawn of a new morning, moving you forward to a new and changed life. As you embrace the forward movement of your changed life, you will once again experience joy and hope in the present and for the future.

CHAPTER ONE
The Story Begins:
Your Loved One Has Died

*T*he story begins with that first phone call. What happened? When? How? And always, Why? These are questions that people seem to need answers to as they learn of the death of a family member, friend, or colleague.

Were you the one receiving or making that call? After the death, the first point of contact is usually via the telephone. The person receiving the call is often in shock just trying to grasp the magnitude of the situation. The person making the call, depending on the closeness to the person who died, is often also in shock and may or may not be able to answer questions about the circumstances surrounding the death. When the death is expected, a plan can be developed and one or two people can be designated to make the calls at the time of death. In cases of sudden death, a family spokesperson and/or close friend usually emerges and that person can make the calls. Each phone call is the beginning of the story for the person on the receiving end, and the retelling of the story for the caller. Do you remember that phone call?

My husband Doug died on December 22, 1996. He was a hospice patient, which allowed us both time to prepare for his death. I had asked my daughter to make the calls at the time of his death. I had a list of names and phone numbers ready. She had helped me prepare the list and we talked about it. But I did not realize the impact that her stepfather's death would have on her. She was in shock and couldn't make any calls. I learned two lessons. The first is to be sensitive to family members and their potential reactions and, the second is the importance of an alternate plan! Even when death is anticipated, loved ones will be at different places in their grief. I can't explain how, just that I was able to rally and start a phone tree. Each person that I called was given at least five people to call. Because my husband's death was expected, the people that I called knew the story and I was able to share with them the very special ending.

One of Doug's last requests was that I would be holding him when he died. I told him that I hoped I could. Since I'd continued working, I wasn't sure I would even be home when he died. That last night I got into bed with him and held him in my arms as I dozed off. When I woke up early the next morning, still holding him, I realized that he had died. The hospice nurse came and the family gathered around us. My son, Rick, put the Christmas music on and when the funeral home staff carried him out, we could hear "Sleep in heavenly peace, sleep in heavenly peace."

The rest of the family came later that day. My son Brian was very upset that my granddaughters didn't get to the house the day before so they could say goodbye. I explained to him that situations have a way of working out. Doug was in and out of consciousness and that may not have been a good memory for the girls. We talked about it as a family and continued to comfort one another. My granddaughters had spent many days with him during the course of his illness. We concluded that it was okay that they weren't with him in his final hours. Family members need to realize it's okay to share feelings and disappointments, which will help you come closer together as a family unit.

The holidays stir up memories for most people as they continue traditions from childhood. When you experience a death at this highly emotional and stressful time of year it can prolong the intensity of your pain. It has been eight years now and I am very happily remarried and still, at times, miss Doug intensely. These times come when I least expect them. Just before Christmas I was in the living room of my former home the year after he died. I was sitting on the sofa across from the spot where Doug's hospice bed had been, and I was reflecting on our last days of December together. My daughter and son-in-law were hosting a family Christmas party and we were singing Christmas carols. I could feel the tears welling up as we started to sing "Silent Night." By the time we got to the chorus the tears were streaming down my cheeks.

A good coping strategy can be to balance your sadness with a fond memory. What helped me at the family gathering was to focus on an earlier fond memory of childhood related to the carol "Silent Night," when the snow was falling gently on my face. It felt refreshing as I watched it fall to the ground and glisten from the reflection of the streetlights. I was walking home from Midnight Mass with my family. We kids were playing in the snow as we heard the church bells in the background. The melody that they were playing was "Silent Night." It seemed like such a perfect night to a thirteen-year-old pondering the Christmas message of peace on earth and remembering the choir at mass singing "Sleep in heavenly peace, sleep in heavenly peace."

This is how the grief process begins—you tell your story. Each time you tell it, it gets a little easier. I once heard that you have to tell your story "nine times ninety-nine and maybe once more." As you tell your story, you help not only yourself, but also all who listen.

When a parent dies it is the loss of the past. As adults, we expect that our parents will die before us. Even though, intellectually, we understand that, it does not make it any less painful. As we grow and mature, our parents become advisors, confidants, and good friends. The pain of that loss is intense and takes time to heal. My mother died when I was in my mid-adult life. I felt comforted by two very special gifts that she had given me. One was my birth and the other was the roots of my faith. However, I was thirteen years old when my father died. He died suddenly so there was no preparation time. I felt the loss deeply. He was away on business and was rushed to a hospital in another city. The next time I saw him was in a coffin at the funeral home. I didn't have a chance to tell him how much I loved him and to say good-bye. This was my first experience with death and so my coping skills were very limited. The grief process takes even longer when one or more of the children are in their teens or younger at the time of their parent's death. The child and teen have not developed the inner resources for coping that an adult has, nor have they been exposed to the life experiences that build coping skills.

At the bereavement camp where I worked, one of the children lost his father in an auto accident. We didn't realize how much he was burdened by guilt until he told the group: "If only I had been with my daddy that day, I could have told him that the truck was coming." This six-year-old was hanging onto a very heavy burden. The camp experience, which included teachings and discussions at the child's level of development, helped him to unload his burden and realize that his daddy's death was not his fault.

The loss of a sibling is the loss of the past, present, and future simultaneously. When a sibling dies, you have lost someone you have spent most of your life with. Your sibling probably knew you better than anyone. You laughed and cried together, plotted and got into trouble together, and protected one another. It was a relationship that will never be forgotten.

I was a young adult when my brother died. I hadn't seen him in two years since he was living out of state. His death was sudden and I never had the chance to say good-bye. Once again the next time I saw my brother was in a coffin at the funeral home. As I looked at him in disbelief, I wanted to say: "Remember when..." I wanted one more chance to laugh and cry with him. Sudden death prevents you from that longed-for time for closure.

I was older when my sister died. We had become close friends. She was a hospice patient so we had some time to say good-bye. It was a different kind of pain than I experienced with the sudden deaths of my father and brother. I remember when we got the call from my brother-in-law. He told Doug and me that the priest had come to see her and it wouldn't be much longer. As we drove from Maryland to Johnstown, New York, I kept saying to myself: "Monica, hang on till I get there." What I felt was her reply: "Connie, I don't think I can and I'm okay." She died an hour before we arrived. In the last few months we had talked about her dying, our relationship, regrets, and fond memories. Even though she died before I arrived, I did feel more of a sense of peace about her death.

For a time after, I remember picking up the phone each week to give her a call, then realizing I couldn't call her—she was dead. When I think of her now, one of my regrets is that we didn't talk more about family history. I still have some blanks in our family story and she was the only one who knew the answers. The bereaved often report the problem of picking up the phone to call a loved one and realizing they cannot. It is those things that we some-times do automatically that quickly bring you back to the reality of your loss, and then the tears flow. I remember that it took some time to remove her name from my address book.

The loss of a child is the loss of the future. As adults we do not expect to bury our children. I remember early in my career as a grief counselor going to the funeral home to be with parents whose child had died from SIDS (Sudden Infant Death Syndrome). As I looked at the small child in the casket, I wanted to pick him up and put him in his mother's arms. It seemed so unnatural to me for them to be separated. The funeral home did make some private time for the parents to hold the child as part of their good-bye. Later, I worked with parents whose teenage son had been murdered. Their pain and anguish was indescribable. They wondered: "Could we survive this?" Their faith was some comfort as they tried to make sense out of two realities: one, that he was dead, and two, that he was murdered. When he left the house that day he was a strong and healthy teen full of life. The parents were often at different places in their anguish, which complicated their ability to comfort one another. This seems to be one of the greatest challenges for parents. It is hard for them to comfort or be comforted. The other children in the family are left floundering. They sometimes wonder if their parents would be in less pain if it had been them who died instead of their brother or sister. Counseling intervention would be appropriate for a family that could not comfort or be comforted by one another.

I have also worked with parents who have lost young adult children. The deaths have followed illnesses, accidents, and other types of trauma. No matter how old or what the cause, your child is not *supposed* to die. We expect them to live from birth to old age. The lesson that I learned is how precious life and family are.

I had one client whose six-year-old daughter died after a long illness. Six months later, I was called to the hospital emergency room by my professional colleague, Betty, because his wife had just died in an auto accident. Betty said she would meet me in the emergency room. I saw her as soon as I got there. Betty had arrived before my client and had helped the staff to prepare the client's wife for viewing. I was having great difficulty controlling my own tears and was at a loss for words, realizing there was *nothing* I could say at that point in time that would comfort him. All I could do was to hold him and cry with him. It occurred to me that working through the grief process is like climbing a mountain, and this man had just fallen all the way down the mountain. Because of my history of knowing his wife and family, I was able to be with him in his pain. He came to realize that the grief, as he understood it, would never really end. But he was able to go on living and, in time, find new meaning and purpose in his life.

One of my own sons was stillborn. He passed out of the birth canal and into the next life in an instant. I found myself taking flowers to his grave on his fortieth birthday, which was also the anniversary of his death. In forty years, I had visited the grave two or three times. I had never taken flowers before or since. My fortieth birthday was a major turning point in my life. I have only recently realized the connection. My youngest son, Michael, went with me to the cemetery that day. He told me that even though he never knew his older brother, he felt a connection to him. In grade school when Michael was asked how many brothers and sisters he had, he would reply that he had one brother who died, two brothers living, and a sister. Bereaved parents will often ask: "How do we answer the question on forms that asks how many children do you have?" Siblings also wonder how to answer the question when it appears on school forms. This is a common issue with many questions surrounding it. After someone dies are they still related? If so when is it appropriate to acknowledge that fact? Each person needs to decide how they will answer when confronted with the question. The bereaved have told me that they do continue to acknowledge the deceased on forms. However, each time they are asked it stirs up the painful feelings of their grief for the first couple of years. After a time they just respond by saying: "I have X number of children living." It's interesting to me that forms do include spousal loss by asking if you are married, widowed, separated, or divorced. Those same forms don't address deceased children or siblings.

At the end of this chapter you will find a worksheet. The purpose of this worksheet is to help you begin to tell *your* story. It can also be used as a tool to help you start your journal. I will say more about the journal in chapter five.

Work Sheet

My _____ died on _____

at _____A.M._____P.M.

He/she was _____ when it happened.

And _____ was with him/her.

How it happened was _____

_____

_____

_____

Why did it happen now at this time in our life

together? _____

_____

_____

What the family needs now from me is _____

_____

_____

What I need now from the family is _____

_____

_____

What I need now from friends is _____

_____

_____

CHAPTER TWO
The Story Continues: How Does Life Get So Out of Balance?

*I*mbalance is defined as the condition of lacking stability. Nothing is the same after a loved one dies. Your world as you knew it moments ago is now changed. Your place in the family changes. Your sense of emotional and financial security is in disarray. Your spirit is shaken by the intensity of the pain.

When death is expected, as in hospice situations, this state of disequilibrium can begin even before the death occurs. It is not unusual to feel conflicted—you are trying to ease your pain by letting go emotionally. It is very difficult to strike a balance between preparing for the impending loss, yet not disconnecting prematurely. This is a time when you realize you have to take one day at a time until you have to take one hour at a time. It is very important for everyone that you remain emotionally and spiritually connected to your loved one until their last breath is taken.

When I tried to focus on my impending loss, the intensity of my pain increased at a time when I needed the emotional energy to be totally present in that moment of our lives. Hospice clients report the most difficulty with this aspect of their grief. The reality is that you do have to begin to plan for how you will manage without your loved one. My husband Doug told me I would have to sell our house and van. I said: "Stop. Wait a minute. I will have plenty of time later after you're gone to deal with those issues." We were at different places with our emotions. He was trying to help me get organized. I was on overload and felt that my life was already changing too quickly. I couldn't contain my tears. He tried to comfort me. This is an example of balance/imbalance. I was able to join with him in the planning once I had some time to process my pain.

At this point, the grieving person is experiencing a total imbalance. Her body is exhausted from twenty-four hour care giving, while her emotions struggle to ease the pain. Intellectually, she is coming to terms with the painful reality of her situation, while spiritually there may be guilt feelings associated with the caregiver's sense of relief that her loved one's struggle will soon be over. The guilt, if left unresolved, can become an issue following the death of her loved one.

Balance is a state of stability of the body or the emotions. The death of a loved one will put you in a state of imbalance. Your physical, emotional, psychological, and spiritual health are affected. You will know something is changing, but you can't put your finger on when it began. What you *do* know is that you feel awful. Henya Kagan describes the need for balance:

> When balance is maintained, it results in an increased energy level and a sensation that the acute pain, which varies in length and intensity, is gradually becoming more tolerable, although it may never entirely disappear....In that respect, the process of readjustment is an evolutionary one—one that continues to evolve and change depending on the type of steps that have been taken.[1]

Grief affects your health in many ways. Try to schedule a complete physical examination during the first month following the death of your loved one so that your physician can help determine whether any symptoms experienced since the death are of a physical or emotional origin. Be sure that the doctor understands that you have just experienced a loss, because your health will be affected at some point. It is important to first rule out any physical cause to your symptoms.

In my case, after my husband died, I had trouble sleeping. I would wake up feeling as though I was gasping for air and concluded that I was having anxiety attacks. For several years my sleep deprivation continued, and I believed it was because I didn't like to be alone at night. After I remarried, my husband noticed that my breathing was very shallow and rapid at night. He also noticed that I had brief periods which looked to him as though I was not breathing at all. I finally checked with my doctor, who ordered a sleep study. I was diagnosed with obstructive sleep apnea! Unknowingly, a serious physical problem remained untreated because I attributed my symptoms to the emotional pain of grief. The lesson that I learned was to practice what I teach, pay more attention to my body, and rule out serious health problems before concluding that their origin is emotional.

Grief affects sleeping and eating patterns for most people. Some want to sleep all the time. This may be a sign of exhaustion or a way of easing their pain. Some can't sleep or sleep is broken up during the night. The bereaved often report that they don't have trouble falling asleep, however, they wake up after two or three hours, and spend the rest of the night awake. Sleep problems are often addressed in support groups. I encourage people to skip napping and instead go to bed at the same time each night. If you find yourself waking up in the middle of the night, try reading or journaling for an hour before going back to bed. Listen to soft music or a relaxation tape. And ask yourself how you handled sleep problems before your loved one died.

Eating is affected when you don't have the interest or energy to prepare a meal. Widowed people find it difficult to eat meals alone. They may eat only junk food. Weight gain or loss is a common problem. I recommend eating five or six small meals rather than three traditional meals. The grief process requires a lot of energy. It is a stressful time in your life. Sleep deprivation and poor nutrition further deplete energy. Adequate sleep and proper nutrition are critical to protecting your immune system, which is already compromised by the stress of grieving. People who have chronic health problems must also be aware that grief is an additional stressor on an already compromised physical condition. Problems such as these are also addressed in bereavement support groups. The bereaved learn from one another what works and what doesn't.

At the time of your loved one's death you will experience feelings of shock and numbness, creating emotional imbalance. These feelings can last from a few moments, to hours, or even days. The *cause* of death is a big factor in how long the feelings last. In the case of sudden death, the numbness protects you for a longer period of time. Many people don't remember too much about the first few days following the death. The wake, funeral, and/or memorial service are often a blur.

In support groups, I review the wake and funeral with the participants as a way of identifying their current support system. We talk about the wake and funeral and who was most and least helpful. Helpfulness is often identified by supportive comments to the bereaved by family and friends. For many, the funeral home is the starting place for their stories. The bereaved display artifacts and pictures that capture the history of the family's and friends' lives with the deceased.

The mother of one of my high school friends died on Christmas Eve. When I went to the funeral home the day after Christmas, what caught my eye first as I approached the casket was the package of M&M's in the coffin with some goodbye notes and drawings from her grandchildren. My friend explained that the M&M's were from the grandchildren because grandma always had M&M's for them when they visited her. This experience taught me that even the very young want to tell their story. Therefore it is important to invite children to participate in the wake and funeral as much as they and their parents feel comfortable with. One of my grandsons had put together a large treasure box of artifacts that reminded him of times shared with his step-grandfather. As people approached the box he would describe each of the treasures to them. It is important to encourage family members to tell their story of the deceased in their own way.

Going to a funeral home and funeral right after Christmas took me back to my story, eight years earlier, on Christmas Eve, and in the funeral home following the death of my husband. I decided to have one of his Christmas traditions at the funeral home. He always had a money tree and the youngest family member got to pick from the tree first; the oldest was the last to pick. Each person had to unwrap his or her little package to see what was received. It was fun; we laughed, and everyone participated.

What I discovered in the telling of my story was that one of my daughters-in-law did not unwrap her little package that year. Instead she saved it and each year since his death she has made it a special ornament on her Christmas tree. We have continued the money tree tradition since then and we remember Doug in a special way each Christmas. This tradition made such an impression on one of my granddaughters that she wrote about it for school. Her essay touched me on many levels. It is about love, loss, moving on, and loving again. Therefore, I have included it at the end of this chapter.

After the funeral people return to their normal routines and you will be left with a painful reality—your loved one is dead and your immediate support network has dispersed. Some will continue to be supportive, while some may not. The numbness is giving way to indescribable pain. The bereaved have described this pain as "though my heart has been ripped out of my chest"; "like a ton of bricks just fell on me and I can't get out from under the pile"; and "I might as well have lost a limb, since a major part of me is gone." The descriptions are images of intense traumatic pain. I encourage clients to describe their pain in images, colors, and sounds. Talking about the pain does help to decrease the intensity. I believe that we can find images to describe our pain when it is difficult to get in touch with our feelings.

Psychological imbalance affects our concentration and decision-making, and also our memory. The bereaved struggle with memory. They clearly remember every detail of their lives with the deceased but they can't remember what they wanted to get at the grocery store. They find that they are consciously working on memory each day. Their attention span is also affected. They have trouble focusing on one task for very long. They may have problems at school or work. One client complained about his memory problems to a friend who replied: "You had memory problems before your wife died." He realized his friend was right! And they were able to laugh about an issue that had been troubling him.

Bereavement groups emphasize helping the griever to stay focused. One strategy is to make lists; another is to give in momentarily when your mind starts to wander by taking a short break. Getting away from the intensity of a situation can help you to refocus and continue with the task at hand. Improving memory requires concentration. A fun way to improve memory is to play games with family and friends, such as board games, cards or word games.

Another way to remain balanced is to maintain your routines. I encourage clients not to make any major changes during the first year if they don't have to. However, some major changes may have already been planned prior to the death and so those plans need to be followed through. One widow reported that her family had just relocated to Maryland from another state. She had two teenaged daughters. Her husband had a massive heart attack and died one month after they moved. Their primary support people were out of state and the girls had left all of their friends behind. They were left with no peer support. Their grief was further complicated because these two major losses occurred within a one-month time frame. You can see from this example that it would not be a good idea to decide to sell a home and relocate shortly after the death of a loved one. It is also not a good idea to redecorate the home, spend large sums of money, or, for the widowed, getting into another permanent relationship. By getting away from the familiar memories, the bereaved believes their pain will be eased, but they later find that their hasty decision-making only delays the healing process. It is important to realize that grieving *actively* is a necessary part of the process. It *cannot* be rushed. Your pain is inside of you and you will take it with you wherever you go. It is like a deep, open wound that heals more completely when left open to heal from the inside out. If you try to close it too quickly it may break open when you least expect it. You will and must grieve. Your choices are *when* and *how.*

A widow came to see me fourteen months after her husband died. She was experiencing feelings of depression and didn't understand why, as she felt that she had done well during the first year following his death. Her family was expressing concern about her frequent tearful outbursts. She just couldn't stop crying. As her story unfolded, it became obvious she had spent that first year after her husband's death comforting family members and taking care of her adult children. Without realizing it, she had spent the last twelve months helping others through their grief instead of getting in touch with her own. The marked change in her behavior in the past few months was an example of delayed grief, which was hard for her and her family to understand. I explained the process and let her know that what she was experiencing was not unusual for her loss. Many widowed clients report that second year is harder than the first. This is true because in the second year, the protective barrier of your numbness has all but disappeared, resulting in feeling the loss of a soul mate more intensely, and the secondary losses in that relationship are more apparent. Some theorists believe as Diane McKissock states:

> It may come as a surprise to encounter clients who say "I could have survived the death of a child, even though I know it would have been unbearably painful, but I can't survive the death of my husband/ wife/ partner." Some partners manage to be lovers, best friends, companions, playmates, colleagues, and co-parents, creating an environment in which they can both develop as individuals, yet create a strong family unit. Their partner may be the only person on earth to know all that they really are; who can accept or appreciate every facet of their being. When a partner dies, it feels like the amputation of a limb.[2]

The McKissocks describe the more immediate secondary losses the deceased played in the life of the bereaved. Just as an amputated limb does not grow back, you cannot regain that relationship. However, amputees do adapt to life without the limb and can move on to sometimes more productive lives. The widowed person, likewise, does adapt to life without the deceased and can move on to a fulfilled life.[3]

In order to help my client with this phase of her sadness, I had her write a letter of good-bye to her husband. I encouraged her to take her time writing the letter, and then to read it out loud to someone and/or bring it to the next session and read it out loud to me. I have learned from the bereaved and my own experience that the letter is therapeutic in that it gives voice to the pain both in the writing and the reading of it out loud.

A good way to begin your letter is with how you have been doing since the death. Include what you miss most, any regrets you may have, and anything you wish you had said prior to the death. Describe how you are coping, what makes you laugh and cry now, as well as any other personal message you would like to include. Use words like *died* or *death* instead of euphemisms such as *left* or *gone*. The words you choose will help you face the reality of the death.

The next step is to decide what to do with the letter. You can decide on one of several options for the letter. Some people keep it for awhile; some decide to bury it at the gravesite; while others burn it and bury the ashes at the gravesite. You may have another idea of what you would want to do with it or how you would want to dispose of it. The suggestions here are what other clients have chosen to do. There is no right or wrong way to do it. There is only what feels right for you and gives closure to any unfinished business contained in the message of the letter.

This is my letter of good-bye. It was written two years after the death of my husband Doug:

Dear Doug,

It's hard to believe that the days turned into weeks, then months, and now years since you died.

I am doing fairly well. I still have my moments when I miss you so intensely that I can hardly stand it. Those times are less frequent now and not as intense.

I have done all the things you encouraged me to do. I sold the van first and split the money with the kids. The Chevy finally died so I had to get a new car.

I paid off the house with the insurance money. You would be happy to know that I recently sold it to Colleen and Vic so it's staying in the family. Also they have a cat. I remember how you loved your cat Rookie.

I have kept in touch with your cousin Connie and her family. Connie is now in assisted living as her eyesight is failing. The rest of your family is doing fairly well.

I left my position at Hospice as you thought I would. I restarted my private practice and continue to do contract work with the college.

What I miss most are our weekends dining out and our trips to Rhode Island and New

Hampshire. I don't get to travel as much anymore. I did get a place at the ocean. You would love it. We spend some time each summer with the kids at the beach.

I miss your smile, your jokes, the way you spoiled me and you were always so proud of my accomplishments.

My only regret is that our life together was cut short.

You said that you hoped I would marry again. I did meet someone and we were recently married. You would be happy to know that I found happiness again.

I have moved forward in my life. I removed your picture from my locket, however you remain in my heart. My new husband was also widowed. We often recall our fond memories of our previous spouses.

I will always miss you. I believe that part of loving you was to honor our life together and move on to love again.

Love, Connie[4]

And here is the essay from our granddaughter Noelle, written about three years after Doug's death:

The Money Tree!!!
We have a tradition in our family that has been going on for seventeen years. It started with my Pop-Pop Doug, but a few years back

he passed away. Now my Mom-Mom just married my Pop-Pop Joe a few years ago, and he has chosen to carry on the tradition that we call "The Money Tree."

We do this tradition on Christmas day after everyone has finished opening their presents. My Pop-Pop Joe will wrap up some ten dollar bills, twenty dollar bills, two fifty dollar bills and one one hundred dollar bill in wrapping paper and put it on a miniature tree. We go from the youngest to the oldest and one at a time pick off of the tree. Some people in my family, like my Uncle Mike, will touch every single wrapping trying to "sense-out" the hundred dollar bill. He got it once, but he was picking for my Uncle that lives in New York, so he didn't get to keep it. Other people, such as me, just go in and snatch the best looking one.

I, of course, like this tradition because I get free money, but I think that my Pop-Pop Joe likes to do this for a much different reason. I think that he likes to do it because he is more fortunate than other people; well, in a way. Pop-Pop Joe had polio when he was only eighteen. It is a disease that only lasts for about a week, but it destroys your nerves and makes it so you can't walk. But he owns his own company and over the years has become fairly successful.

I think that in his later years, it makes him happy to be able to make other people happy. It is sort of like he knows he has fulfilled his life's dream, and he is trying to help other people fulfill theirs. It is like it makes him proud. Even if he is just helping a little at a time.

—by Noelle Kline[5]

CHAPTER THREE
The Story Helps
You Hold It All Together

*T*he facts in your story keep you grounded while the feelings it stirs in you help in the healing. What I refer to as your support system may be one or several people. They may be family, friends, colleagues, clergy, counselors, and/or support groups. These people are available to you for a time after the death. Most support networks are in place in varying degrees for at least a year. As I've stated before, what has become more apparent in recent years is that the second year is often reported to be harder than the first, which may feel like a setback. I believe that happens because the numbness is truly gone, so you will feel your feelings more intensely.

I also believe that if you pay attention to your grief during the first year and lean into your pain, the second year will be a little easier.

Clients have stated: "My family and friends say that I have to stop feeling sorry for myself. I have to snap out of it and go on with my life. I am making everyone around me miserable. My sadness brings them down. They don't know how to help me anymore. They say that I need professional help and that is why I am here." I can't count the times that this has been the introduction of the presenting problem. Clients usually come to see me within six to nine months following the death.

When the griever hears the words "feeling sorry for myself," what they may then feel is guilt and a sense of letting the important people in their life down. They are terrified of losing their support network, so they conclude that they have to change their behavior as soon as possible. They have come to see me, the counselor, so that I can tell them how to do that. They think that they will be able to stop the pain, change, and get on with life. It would be nice if the process were that simple! Unfortunately, that kind of thinking will only delay and prolong the grieving process.

What the bereaved needs help in understanding is that family and friends are speaking out of their own frustration. They don't know *how* to help. They themselves are feeling helpless. It is difficult to watch a loved one in pain and not be able to help them. I explain that family and friends are very concerned and are trying to help in the only way they know how.

Remember, too, that you have to let people know what you *need*. You also should let them know that you are okay even when you cry. In the beginning of this book, you learned that *you* are the primary teacher and the lesson is your story. It is therefore appropriate for you to assume the responsibility for your healing. You will now teach your loved ones about your need for their patience, as you cannot rush the process.

It is good to get additional help during this time so that you do not exhaust your current support people and you don't try to do it alone. You can add on to your support system at any time. Remember that your family and friends are also feeling the pain of the loss in their own way. The support group is a good additional resource for learning about the grief process and realizing that you are not losing control, going crazy or doing it all alone. There are others who feel as you do. Most support groups are limited to six weeks in length. The groups have a threefold format. During the first two weeks the focus is on the awareness of their loss. These first two weeks are the hardest for the griever, who is already in a vulnerable state and tends to absorb the pain of others in the group as they tell their stories. I explain to participants that it is not unusual to feel *worse* during these first two weeks, but that the intensity will subside as they move into the third week of the group. I find that when we explain this to the bereaved they are more inclined to trust the process and stay with the group. Leaders encourage grievers to tell their stories and share photographs of their deceased loved one. The photos are a way for group members to get a better sense of one another's losses, as they now have a face to go with the story that they are hearing.

The middle two weeks of the group focus on coping. There is more active teaching by the leaders and interaction between group members as they learn general coping skills. Problems in coping are identified by participants, while leaders and other group members give suggestions on how to improve coping skills.

The last two weeks of the group focus on moving on in life as you embrace and incorporate your loss. The leaders explain that the process will *not* be over in six weeks, but what *will* be different is that participants will have a better understanding of the feelings they have been experiencing. They will know more about the grief process and they will have learned some additional and useful coping skills. Also, they may have made some new friends in the group.

In one of my support groups there was a woman who lost her father. When she introduced herself and started her story, she said that she was doing okay but her mother wasn't. It had been a year since her father's death and her mother wasn't coping well. She came to the group to learn how to help her mother. I noticed that she listened intently to the widows in the group tell their stories and describe their coping skills. By the end of the first session, the woman realized her mother was doing fine and *she* was the one who needed to be in the group! She was the one who was not coping well. After hearing the four widows and another daughter speak, she realized that her mother's grief was quite appropriate. This goes to show that support groups of mixed grievers do help family members to see how other family members are coping. The widows in the group that day also realized why their own children were responding to them with some concerns. People in support groups learn valuable lessons from other members of the group that they can apply to their own current situations.

Another woman in my support group reported that she was finally able to let go of her husband's clothes. She had them all packed up and ready to go. When the Goodwill staff came to pick them up she was ready. Then, suddenly, she asked for one of the bags back and grabbed a sweater out of it. It was her husband's favorite sweater and she realized that she wasn't ready to let go of it just yet. I affirmed for her that it was okay to hang on to it. I reassured her that when she was ready she would let go of it. There is no time frame for getting rid of the clothes and other belongings of the deceased. Each person has to do it in his or her own time. As I relate this story, I am reminded of my husband's Snoopy sweater that I was not ready to part with when the Disabled American Veterans came to pick up his clothes. I would wear the sweater on the cold winter nights when I missed him intensely. However, I did let it go several months later when I could replace it with the warmth of summer.

Getting rid of the clothes and belongings is a very personal matter. When the time is right for you, you will do it. The balance is in knowing when to hang on and when to let go. Family members express concern when another family member turns a bedroom or other part of the home into a "shrine" to the deceased. This happens more often when the deceased is a child. I have heard parents say that the death of their child caused them to be frozen in time as though the clock had stopped. I believe that this is what shock and numbness can do. Since the child will not continue to develop and grow, the "shrine" may evolve as a way of keeping that moment in time frozen and undisturbed. I have learned that the grief process takes longer to move through when you're dealing with the death of a child. Other parents who have lost a child may have suggestions for how to continue to acknowledge your child's short life. For instance, consider ways to change a room into a living memory that would honor the child that died, such as a place to play, have fun, or be creative.

Remember, you may need some additional help in processing ways to incorporate your loss as you make decisions about the belongings of the deceased. This is one of the benefits in participating in a support group.

Keep in mind that support groups are *not* for everyone. If you are a person who went through a group and didn't feel helped by it or you just don't feel comfortable sharing your feelings in a group setting you will need other suggestions for support. I would suggest you talk to a friend who is going through a similar experience. Another option is to consider some short-term individual sessions with a grief counselor.

My husband, Joe, mapped out a four point plan that helped him following the death of his first wife. These four points simultaneously helped him to move forward and stay balanced during a very difficult time in his life.

- You pray for the physical and emotional strength to cope with what you have to cope with.
- Don't make any major changes in your life routines. Go to the same places that you and your spouse did and with the same people, for example going out to dinner or to the theater.
- Stay as busy as you can so that you don't have too much time to dwell on your loss.
- Be as nice to people as you can while they are alive so you have few, if any, regrets, and honor the dead by taking good care of the living.[6]

He has also helped other widowers by explaining this strategy to them. He continues to help other grievers one-on-one. A support group was not an option he felt comfortable with. The men he has helped have come back to thank him for helping them get "unstuck" and being able to move on with their lives. We do know that men and women handle grief differently.

Tom Golden writes: "Grief is a problem without an easy solution. When anyone confronts a problem that has no solution he or she will often feel lost. When a woman feels lost, she tends to ask for help. When a man feels lost, he looks for maps."[7] Tom has learned that men need a different definition to help them understand their grief. "Terms like *chaos* and *desire* will supplant the usual definitions of grief in terms of feelings."[8]

Golden also states an interesting observation:

> Death professionals have long been con-
> founded by the difference between men
> and women in visiting gravesites. The
> men tend to visit more often. Men tend
> toward linking their grief with a place,
> action or thing. There are many exam-
> ples: the man whose daughter died, who
> wore her ring as a remembrance of her;
> the man who carved a bust of his wife
> after her death; a man who built a pond
> in memory of his murdered brother; a
> man who wore his father's watch; and, on
> and on.[9]

Women, however, most often link their grief with
emotions, and then share those emotions with supportive
people who love them. Although they use different strategies, both men and women find ways to regain balance in
their lives. Golden cautions:

> It needs to be said that when we divide
> men and women into two distinct groups,
> we are in dangerous territory. All people
> are unique in the ways they find to heal
> themselves. There are probably more indi-
> vidual differences in grief than there are
> gender differences, but the gender differ-
> ences do exist and need to be honored.[10]

Another issue of balance is learning when to focus on yourself and when to reach out and help others. People who are grieving often believe that volunteering will help them "get over" their grief. This is not always the case, especially when it comes to volunteering in a hospice. Many people who want to become hospice volunteers have experienced a recent death loss. We are able to identify their readiness to volunteer at the time of the interview and during training. If you want to volunteer in a hospice, part of the training procedure will involve evaluating how much you have resolved your own story of loss. The hospice families can and will unknowingly trigger your own pain. If you have not healed sufficiently, that trigger will render you unable to be a helper in this environment. You must first deal with your own unfinished business through peer support and/or counseling. One to two years is usually sufficient time after a death to become a hospice volunteer.

For some of the recently bereaved, reaching out and helping others is what energizes them. In that case, you should pursue other volunteer efforts such as soup kitchens, Meals-on-Wheels, or literacy programs that can all be done simultaneously with your grief work. Then you can reach out to others while caring for yourself at the same time.

There are other ways to maintain balance in your life. For those who are uncomfortable with the idea of support groups or not ready to volunteer, many books on grief topics have been written by people following the death of their loved one. Some of these books may have started as journals. Look for books that either address grief in general or cover issues specific to your story. If you are widowed, you will want to read on that specific topic. There are also books about coping with the loss of a parent and the loss of a child. Several movies address the topic of grief. Some hospice bereavement services include a movie night that is open to the public. A movie on grief will be followed by a general discussion on how the movie may have touched the audience. Bereaved people have reported that these programs have been very helpful to them. I have provided a listing of resources at the end of this chapter.

When your tears remain so out of control that they interfere with your daily functioning, or you find you are withdrawing from people and that it has become easier to isolate yourself some aspect of your sadness is out of balance. If this happens, you may want to consider some individual counseling sessions. The counselor can help you identify your strengths in coping and suggest ways to access them when you're feeling totally out of control. The grief process also triggers the pain of past losses that may be unresolved.

I like the way Tom Golden describes the difference between grief and depression. He says grief is the ability to:

> ...stand in our own tension arising from a loss. It is the natural response to a normal life experience. Many times when a depressed person begins to feel what is inside—not the negative thought processes but the feelings within—they are starting to heal themselves. The distinction can

get a bit complicated, but the general rule is that grief is related to the acknowledgement, honoring, and often expression of feeling connected to a loss, and depression is a form of pathological negative thinking.[11]

You will come to recognize these past losses as they relate to your current loss and work through them toward healing. The writing of this book has stirred up many feelings related to my past losses. As the feelings emerge I continue to address them through the retelling of my story, in my journaling, and through peer support.

Movies

Angels in the Outfield
Bridge of Terabithia
Casper
Heidi
My Girl
Snow White
The Sound of Music
Three Lives of Thomasina
The Trouble With Angels
The Notebook

Books

Living With Grief After Sudden Loss edited by Kenneth Doka, Jr.

Coping With Grief in My Own Way: The Bereavement Journal by Diane and Mel McKissock

Grief Climb Toward Understanding by Phyllis Davies

A Grief Observed by C. S. Lewis

How to Take Care of You by Sue Vineyard

CHAPTER FOUR
The Story Is
Laughter and Tears

emember that every laugh starts with a smile. "Smiles is the longest, shortest, and quickest word in the English language. You probably know why it is the longest—because there is a mile between the first and last letter. It is also the shortest, because a smile is an instant communicator, and the quickest because a smile is the swiftest way to get rid of your doldrums."[12]

How can a person be in the midst of deep sadness and be able to laugh? Although grief itself may not be funny, some life situations are often very funny and while you are grieving you are also in the midst of *living*. Some people in pain need permission to laugh. They feel guilty if they are having a good time. Have you ever laughed so

hard that your laughter brought tears to your eyes, or cried so hard that you ended up laughing? The great Irish writer James Joyce once called these "laughtears"—and "funerals" Joyce renamed "funforalls."

"In early childhood development, a smile precedes a laugh. Babies smile within the very first week after birth; laughter is not evident until about the third or fourth month." Dr. David Bresler, former director of the pain control unit at the University of California, strongly believes laughter is therapeutic and "...therefore, starts with the predecessor to a laugh, a smile, and encourages his patients to move away from their pain by smiling. He even writes prescriptions for his patients that direct them to go to the mirror and smile twice an hour."[13]

Your laughter and tears come from the same place in your emotions. Tears and laughter are two of the most important healing tools for you now.

I have often described grief to be like swimming under water. When you swim under water you have to come up for air periodically. Laughter is a griever's way of coming up for air. Picture the absurdity of trying to laugh under water. You won't be able to stay under for very long. Whether swimming under water or in the depths of your worst grief, laughing will bring you up. It is nothing to feel guilty about. It relaxes and is very healing. Don't allow yourself to continuously feel the intense pain of your loss and believe it to be unending. Grief-work is exhausting and you will need periodic episodes of laughter.

I remember when my son died. The only relief I felt from the pain was the daily reruns of the *I Love Lucy* show. I felt as though the antics of Lucy and Ethel were providing some respite from the almost intolerable pain. I would laugh so hard that my incision hurt, as I was also recovering from a caesarean section. I found myself looking forward to the half hour of fun each day in those months after his death.

The funniest stories I have heard from bereaved people have been about problems in coping with day-to-day situations. The situations were not funny at the time, but only later during the retelling of the experience.

Here is an example from my own experience. The winter after my husband's death I was trying to use our snowblower to clear the driveway so I could get the car out to go to work. I don't know exactly what or how I did it, but very quickly, I was almost buried in the snow. All I could do at the time was cry and yell: "Doug, where are you when I need you?" My neighbor heard my crying and came to my rescue. As he listened to my tale of woe, he started laughing. He apologized for his laughter by saying, "I'm sorry, but you look like a cartoon." When he said that, I started to laugh, too! He got me out of the snow pile, cleared the driveway with my snowblower, and I went off to work. When I got to work, my colleagues also found my story to be very humorous.

One widow in our group became very upset when her refrigerator stopped working. Unsure of what to do, she hollered for her husband: "John, where are you when I need you?" The doorbell rang. She answered and her *son* John Jr. was at the door! He was making a surprise visit and had heard her calling out, so when she opened the door he said: "You called—I'm here." They embraced and started laughing. That day he felt a need to stop by and see his mother and he had arrived at just the right moment.

My friend and colleague, who was trying to "keep it all together" after her husband died, was running late for an important meeting at work. The pool man had come to clean the pool. As she was getting out the equipment for him she stepped too near the edge of the pool. She tripped and fell in—as she put it—"panty hose and all." She got out of the pool—makeup dripping, hairdo ruined, and soaked to the skin. She said she had two choices: to laugh or to cry. She chose to laugh, as tears would only further ruin her makeup. First she called the office to delay the meeting. When she arrived an hour later and relayed her excuse, the whole room was filled with laughter. She said it turned out to be a very good day.

These stories are examples of leaning into the pain while choosing the healing power of laughter. Patsy Clairmont, who is known for her wit and wisdom, has a way of helping women to see that laughter is sometimes the best medicine for the soul. Her books and presentations emphasize the importance of laughter in our lives:

> Laughter can make moments more memorable. Whether laughing alone or with others, it helps us feel good about our memories. Laughter is an incredible gift. It helps us to not take ourselves too seriously and makes it possible for us to survive life's awkward moments.[14]

Remember to give yourself permission to laugh. It's good medicine for the body and soul. Consider what triggers your laughter. For me it's thinking about some of the antics of my grandchildren. I find that I smile when I think of them and I laugh with them whenever we're together.

CHAPTER FIVE
The Story as Recorded in the Journal

As you journey through the experience of grief the journal will become an important tool for assessing your progress. In support groups and seminars I have described it as a measuring tool. A daily journal allows you to look back and identify patterns in actions and behaviors. For instance, you will find during the first year that several consecutive days or even weeks will pass where you think you are coping well and doing fine, then suddenly you will experience a surge of intense grief. This occurrence is natural and expected, although when it happens you will feel that you have taken a huge step backward in your healing. Reviewing the previous entries in your journal will help you to see that you haven't gone backward. You just hit a bump in the road.

The journal is your personal dialogue with yourself. Daily writing will become a habit and help you stay balanced. It can also tap into your personal creativity. Rereading previous entries will let you examine situations to see if you have set realistic expectations for yourself. Over time, different themes in your pain and patterns of coping will emerge in your recordings. It may well surprise you how much better you will know yourself after the experience of journaling.

Although every person grieves differently, there are many predictable situations and milestones you will face. Therese Rando feels that, in general, most people underestimate the length and severity of their bereavement. Our expectations tend to be too unrealistic, and more often than not we receive insufficient assistance from friends and society. Your grief will not only be more intense than you expected but it will also be manifested in more areas and ways than you ever anticipated. You can expect to see brief upsurges of it at anniversary and holiday times, and in response to certain stimuli that remind you of what you have lost. Your grief will be very different from others' and dependent upon the meaning of your loss, your own personal characteristics, the type of death, your social support, and your physical state.[15] A journal will help you contemplate these situations and allow you to stay balanced and in control. Following are some journal entries that will serve as examples to help you get started.

A page from Linda's journal:

March 3, 1959

It's 6:30 A.M. on a Friday morning. A very vivid memory of my mother's death (phone ringing, followed by screams and sobbing). I am barely awake and my mother's best friend, Agnes, is standing over my bed and tells me through her tears that my mother has just died. I am desperately trying to grasp what I just heard. She only had a bad cold when she went to the hospital. She is supposed to come home today. Agnes tells me that my mother's only kidney collapsed and she died.

I remembered my mother's last words as she left for the hospital. She told us to obey our grandmother and we did. My two siblings and I, one two months old and the other nine. I was twelve years old. I dealt with it by pretending that my mother was still in the hospital, that she had TB and was up in the mountains.

I recall my fondest memory of my mother. It was Christmastime the year before she died. My mother, grandmother, and I cooked the Christmas dinner together. My mother taught me to make fudge. I bought her a pair of earrings for Christmas. She was buried in them. I wished I would have been able to get her a more beautiful pair since it was my last Christmas gift to her.

I recall my grief lasting through junior high and high school. After my mother's death, there was very little talk of her around the house. When my father died my brother reminded me of that. He wished we had told him some stories about our mother so that he would have felt that he knew her.

My grandmother would often say to us growing up that God doesn't give us any more than we can bear. As I reflect back now in my adult life, I regret that I did not share my memories of my mother with my younger siblings. Now I would advise anyone who loses a loved one to talk about the person and your feelings about the loss. It will keep the memories alive and help younger family members to more actively share in their loss.[16]

Linda was very young when her mother died and her siblings were even younger. Starting a journal at *any* point in your sadness is therapeutic. It helps you to recapture the essence of the story and the feelings connected to your loss experience. We know that when a young child loses a parent they will grieve again as they approach each of their developmental milestones. These include first date, first job, first child, graduations, weddings, job promotions, special vacations, and the like. Linda's grief experience has had a positive effect in her adult life, as she helped to start a bereavement support program in her church. She knows the pain firsthand and now she ministers to others in her faith community.

The journal is a valuable tool for the grieving person. I encourage *all* of the bereaved that I work with to write in a journal. I encourage them to make daily entries. It can be an account of the day, a challenging experience that was faced, or just one word, a line on the page, or even the sentence, "I don't have anything to say." The point is to become disciplined enough to open the journal each day and not to worry about entries. It will provide some daily structure. Grief can feel very chaotic and out of control, and you can restore some measure of order to your life by beginning or ending your day or both with this small ritual. You will soon find that you look forward to the moments with your journal. The words and tears will start to flow.

My journal started with the following entry:

> *This will be the story of my first year following the death of my husband Doug and my good friend and colleague Betty. The pain is intense.*

Following are two excerpts from that first year. The first entry was written twelve weeks after his death:

> *Sunday, March 16*
> *It has been twelve weeks since Doug died. I'm still tearful. I had mixed feelings about going out to dinner with friends last evening. I was*

surprised that I did enjoy myself. Now I have to face the challenge of filing taxes without you, Doug. I'm wondering how much I'll have to pay and will I have enough. Finances are of continuous worry as I struggle to make it on my own. I don't like being alone. I don't like the pain of grief. I knew it was coming but didn't know exactly how it would feel. I wonder what it will be like next March. Is the second year really harder than the first?

I'm going to celebrate St. Patrick's Day tomorrow somehow, somewhere—even if I have to do it alone. I miss you, Doug. You would be celebrating with me. I love you soooo much.

I've mentioned that holidays and special occasions can be painful reminders of the special times you shared with your loved one, and the above entries demonstrate the intensity of that pain. The stirring of these memories will be difficult for you, but it is what allows the tears to flow. The next entry was written about ten months after his death:

Friday, October 31
I went to bed in tears and woke up in tears. I remember last Halloween—Doug's last. He wanted to greet the trick-or-treaters and give the candy. He was enjoying what we both knew was his last Halloween. Today was more

painful than I expected. Went to see my son
perform. I started to cry as he was singing. I
want Doug here with me. I miss him so much.
The tears just keep coming.[17]

There are many types of diaries and journals available in any bookstore. Colorful and filled with pictures or plain and unlined—choose the journal that appeals to you. The book I chose that first year was *Journeying Through the Days*. My journal had calendar pages with space set aside for personal reflections. It also had a daily spiritual meditation printed at the top of each page, which got me in touch with the spiritual pain of my grief.[18]

When I look back now I can see how far I've come. The words of Bishop Calvin D. McConnell were a great inspiration in helping me to get started: "As we go into our year, may our reflective journaling enable us to discover promises and possibilities that await us all in our companionship with God, the Son and the Holy Spirit."[19]

This is why a journal is so necessary to the healing process. Grieving is often described as a roller coaster ride or like waves in the ocean, because when you reach the low points you feel as though you have just been thrown back to square one in the process. This is where your journal is most useful—you can look back at your journal entries and realize that you are *not* back at the beginning, rather, you have actually made progress.

CHAPTER SIX
The Story Includes
Spiritual Pain

*A*s you begin to move forward, let the story return you to the roots of your faith. Earlier in this book I acknowledged my faith as one of the special gifts I received from my mother. This is your *faith story.*

Spirituality relates to the core of your being, often referred to as your soul. I believe that we are all spiritual and some of us are also religious. We connect to people through our spirit and we say we've found our soul mate. Our beliefs and values come from our spirituality. The roots of your faith are spiritual and may contain some teachings from the religious beliefs of your parents. Therefore the pain of grief will affect your spirit and cause you to question the true meaning of life. You begin to

make sense out of it when your intellect and spirit come together as you integrate the loss.

Even though intellectually we understand that death is a part of life, the timing is *never* right. We all hope for long and healthy lives. Then we learn that death has no age. It can come to the fetus, the full-term stillborn, the infant, toddler, child, teen, and adult at any age. It can be anticipated, as in some illnesses, or sudden, like the proverbial thief in the night. Whenever it comes it brings pain that touches the very core of your being. The pain is so deep that it pierces your heart and soul.

Henri Nouwen describes the weeks following his mother's death noting that "fatigue, sorrow, sadness and confusion were certainly part of it, but also a joy, gratitude, new insights and beautiful memories. I had to fight the temptation to 'get back to normal' too soon." Nouwen describes balancing his pain with fond memories of his mother. His ability to be in touch with sad and happy emotions simultaneously reminds us of the importance of giving equal time to our laughter and tears, as discussed in the previous chapter.[20]

Johanna Turner, in her book, *Grief and Faith*, writes:

> This is your faith story, and this is the time to remember it. Gather these memories and think about them often. What you learned from them may be challenged by your loss, and some of your faith memories may not be good ones. But it is your story nonetheless, and it is the foundation

for accepting and strengthening God's presence in your life.[21]

Spiritual pain asks the "Why?" questions. Why did this happen to me at this point in my life? Why did my loved one suffer for such a long time? Why do young children lose one or both parents? I'm sure there are as many answers as there are people to ask these questions. The six-year-old wondered why his daddy didn't see the truck coming. The parents wondered why their young healthy son was murdered. Some responses grievers find comforting, others, they do not.

The spiritual pain of grief can then be described as a loss of meaning and purpose. Whatever role our loved one played in our lives, that person is now gone and we cannot get that time back. One of our tasks in grief is to redefine ourselves in the world and to decide how we will reestablish meaning and purpose in our lives. From a christian perspective, Henri Nouwen was able to work through his spiritual pain by making his mother:

> ...a participant in God's ongoing work of redemption by allowing her to dispel in me a little more of my darkness and lead me a little closer to the light. In these weeks of mourning she died in me more and more every day, making it impossible for me to cling to her as my mother. Yet by letting her go I did not lose her. Rather, I found that she is closer to me than ever. In and

through the spirit of Christ, she indeed is becoming a part of my very being.[22]

When Betty, my friend and professional colleague died unexpectedly, I felt a crushing blow to my spirit. She was a close friend who had been my primary support person during my husband's illness. The last day that I was able to talk with her she came to my house to witness some changes in our will. The next time I saw her, she was in a coma in an intensive care unit. Betty died twelve days before my husband. She was not supposed to die. I didn't get a chance to say good-bye. Why did it happen to her at this time in her life? Her family still needed her. I still needed her. She and I traveled the United States together as we presented programs on grief to other professionals and to grieving people. She was responsible for starting the hospice bereavement camp for children. The camp was born out of her own grief story. When her first husband died, there were no programs to help her little boy with the sudden death of his daddy.

The camp was named Camp Nabe (pronounced "knobby"), the Korean word for butterfly or moth. It was one of the first bereavement camps for children in Maryland. I remember that very first session when we both saw a white butterfly fly across the field where the children were gathered. We both thought, at the same time, that the butterfly was God's messenger to let us know that He was smiling on the camp. The children saw it too; one of the children said: "Look Nabe, you have a little buddy." From that moment, we realized that the camp was, for us, a grief ministry.

After Betty died, my husband Doug also felt the loss deeply and, as sick as he was, wanted to attend her funeral. He expressed concern for me, in that I had just lost a major part of my support network. After my friend's passing, I was on grief overload. It was impossible to deal with Betty's death while continuing my dual role as wife and primary caregiver to my terminally ill husband. At a time when I needed to be able to pause and reflect, I had to keep going. But the situation became too overwhelming. I was only able to cope by putting my grief for Betty on hold for a year. I planned a brunch to honor the first anniversary of her death. It was in the planning of that brunch that I started to actively grieve her loss. I put a memory book together for her family and titled it "Remembering Betty." I asked all of the people invited to the brunch to submit a memory. Even people who were not able to attend the brunch sent a memory for the booklet. It was a very healing experience for me as I laughed and cried while reviewing the memories and assembling the memory book. Many people who attended commented that it helped them to bring closure to their grief. Betty's family was very grateful for the continued outpouring of love for their mother and the treasure of the memory book. Betty was a deeply spiritual person who touched my spirit from the moment I first met her. I still miss her and I think I always will.

Funerals and memorial services address your spiritual pain. In describing the funeral director's role at the time of loss, Steve Sunderland states "death is divine and life is divine, and that funeral director is right at the center of this divinity, of this sacredness. The griever is at a point of transition. The funeral director has a key role to honor the wishes of the deceased as expressed by the family and to maintain a caring environment in the funeral home."[23] Many families decide to have the service right in the funeral home. The service may include the religious component of your spirituality, depending on the wishes expressed by the deceased prior to death. Each religion has its own traditions and rituals with prayers and music to help the mourner move through the process.

Hospices hold annual nondenominational memorial services to honor the families of all patients who died within the past year. It is a healing ritual for staff, volunteers, and families and friends of the deceased. Refreshments are served after the service. Sometimes it is a potluck supper where the bereaved are asked to fix the favorite dish of their loved one. This is a bittersweet time for all.

At some point, many clients who find themselves "stuck" in their grief identify feelings of anger and guilt as spiritual pain. When the client feels that the anger is getting out of control, it increases their feelings of guilt. The anger may be directed outwardly or kept inside. These feelings stir up your spiritual pain.

Anger often relates to your feelings of unfairness concerning your present situation and fears about the future. Anger needs to be heard and acknowledged as a legitimate feeling. Once acknowledged, it also needs to be expressed. You will need to find a healing outlet for the intense feelings. Dr Elisabeth Kübler-Ross would have a mattress at her training seminars with a piece of rubber hose for the person to beat the mattress with. The exercise provided a constructive physical outlet for some very intense feelings.[24] Anger is a legitimate feeling that needs to be expressed in a way that is safe for all concerned. Once anger is expressed in a way that does not harm anyone, the griever experiences some relief from the spiritual pain.

Guilt also weighs you down. Ask yourself: "What am I guilty of? What did I do that is so unforgivable?" It is important that you talk with your priest, rabbi, minister, or counselor about these feelings. He or she will help you to put them in perspective and begin to forgive yourself so you can move forward with a heavy burden lifted.

Reverend Gilbert states:

> Our "task" in life as the bereaved is to give meaning to the world, and our place in this world, after everything has been changed or rewritten. Sometimes we believe that God has been changed, or that God's words (or Word) has been rewritten, and that we have been written out of God's plans. It is in those moments of deepest hurt, and as we risk our deepest honesty, that we can discover that God is still walking in our shoes, listening to our stories and affirming us in our pain.[25]

CHAPTER SEVEN

The Story Concludes When You Take the "U" out of Mourning and Move Into the Dawn of a New Morning

*D*uring this mourning time the focus has been on you, the mourner. It has been a time when you needed to take special care of yourself. Grief-work emphasizes the need for self-care. While this focus on self-care seems exaggerated at times, it is part of trying to keep some balance in a very unbalanced experience

Over time, you will start to realize that you are feeling better. Physically you have more energy. Keep that energy positive through an exercise program. You find that you are looking forward to each new day with some anticipation. Your interest in others has returned. Nurture that interest by reaching out to help others. You may now be ready to volunteer. Psychologically you know that you are

thinking more clearly and you are able to concentrate for longer periods of time. You are now ready to take a second look at the many decisions that had been on hold and make the decisions that will continue to improve the quality of your life.

You realize that you have survived many firsts without the deceased, such as birthdays, anniversaries, holidays, and other special occasions. You find that the time leading up to those dates was usually more painful than the actual date.

The tears are not gone, thank God. They are more spaced out and when they come, they don't feel uncontrollable. Remember that tears are *good*. They bathe the eyes and remove toxins from the body. Emotionally you feel stronger and much more in control of those tears. Spiritually, you now realize that God never left; you were not abandoned. Though it may have felt like it, you were never truly alone in your grief. Your faith may have been the main force in your life that sustained you in your darkest hours. All the more reason to rejoice now as you celebrate each and every new morning. Take time to smile and be thankful for each new day.

My faith did sustain me during my times of grief. After my husband's death, the first thing I did to take care of myself was to go on a retreat. I needed to take myself out of the mainstream of my daily life and spend some time in quiet prayer and reflection to center myself. I left the retreat feeling stronger knowing that I would not be alone. Through my faith, I knew my God was with me and would remain constant, but when I hit some of the rough spots in my grief I would still cry out: "Where are you God? I need you now."

After the retreat I made plans to visit my friends in Florida for a much needed rest. They were able to balance the time of my visit between giving me space and pampering me. I had no idea how truly exhausted I was until I began to relax and let myself feel the healing warmth of the sun. It was another valuable healing experience in the grief process.

It's been quite a journey. There were days when you wondered how you would survive. It was a struggle just getting out of bed each day. You wondered just how much more intense the pain could get. Then it did get worse. You were, at times, overwhelmed by your fear of facing yet another day without your loved one. You thought the tears would never stop. There were times you felt exhausted as you struggled to hide your feelings to protect others from your grief. Your problems with memory and concentration got in the way of functioning at home, school, and work. Hopefully you were surrounded by understanding people who were patient with you. You appreciated the caring concern of family, friends, and co-workers but knew that they really had no way of knowing what you were going through. That realization only intensified your feelings of aloneness.

This new dawn of morning has not been a *sudden* change. It has evolved through the experience of the healing process. It started with the first moment of your mourning and continued until this new morning. Your spirit has awakened to the newness of this day. Now is the time to consider *What Brings You to Life*. Bev Eanes, Lee

Richmond, and Jean Link posed that question to women in their book of the same name. "Whether you are learning to connect with yourself or deepening your connection with others and with God, you will become more in tune with the rhythms of the universe. As you discover your dance of life, you will find more space to relax, more freedom to move at your own pace and more time for creative ideas and feelings to penetrate your heart and soul."[26]

The following reflection of Macrina Wiederkehr was an inspiring prayer for me during my grief journey:

> I like to be awake when morning arrives,
> ready to be faithful to the possibility she
> brings. I want to be waiting for her, open
> to receive the gift that she is. I pray for
> everyone who, at this moment, is receiv-
> ing the gift of morning.

> The East is getting out her gold
> She holds it out against the night
> And scatters darkness
> With her light.
> Then morning comes
> Climbing over the hill
> Like an eager, restless child.
> She pauses just a moment
> Then casts her color on the earth.

> Morning, color me bright
> I've been afraid too long

The color of fear is dark
Darker than night
But your glance is full of light.

Don't hurry morning;
Come slowly.
Dress yourself in light.
Climb over that hill lovingly
Hand me a new day hopefully
Get into my bloodstream, and
Color me like the rising sun
Slowly
I've a mind to be contagious
Color me bright.

Your story continues to be told and retold whether you are talking to God or one another. Wiederkehr's prayerful reflections touch my story of healing. She refers to it as "The Sacrament of Hope."[27] Hope is that new life force that we embrace as we move from mourning to morning. On that new morning a new story begins and so the circle of life continues with each new day.

Notes

Chapter 2

1. Henya Kagan, *Gili's Book* (New York: Teachers College Press, 1998), 128.

2. Dianne McKissock and Mal McKissock, *Bereavement Counseling* (South Australia: Griffith Press, 1998), 102.

3. Ibid.

4. Constance Mucha, journal entry, December 2002.

5. Noelle Kline, journal entry, 8 November 2003.

Chapter 3

6. Joseph Mucha, letter to author, 22 February 2004.

7. Tom Golden, "A Man's Grief," *M.E.N. Magazine* (November 1994).

8. Ibid.

9. Tom Golden, "A Tree for My Father," *M.E.N. Magazine* (March 1996).

10. Ibid.

11. Golden (1994).

Chapter 4

12. Allen Klein, *The Healing Power of Humor* (Los Angeles: Jeremy P. Tarcher, Inc., 1989), 95.

13. Ibid., 96.

14. Patsy Clairmont et al., *Humor for a Woman's Heart* (West Monroe, LA: Howard Publishing Co., 2001), 70.

Chapter 5

15. Therese A. Rando, *Grieving: How to Go on Living when Someone You Love Dies* (Lexington, MA: Lexington Books, 1988), 79.

16. Linda Simmons, journal entry, June 2000.

17. Constance Mucha, journal entries, 2002.

18. Bishop Calvin D. McConnell, Introduction, *Journeying Through the Days 1997* (Nashville: The Upper Room, 1996).

19. Ibid.

Chapter 6

20. Henri J.M. Nouwen, *In Memoriam* (Notre Dame, IN: Ave Maria Press, 1980), 57.

21. Johanna Turner, *Grief and Faith* (Washington, DC: American Hospice Foundation, 1997), 9.

22. Nouwen, 60.

23. Steve Sunderland, "Funeral Director's Role at the Time of Loss," *American Funeral Director Newsletter* 9 (1992): 20.

24. Elisabeth Kübler-Ross, *To Live Until We Say Goodbye* (Englewood Cliffs, NJ: Prentice-Hall, Inc., 1978), 58.

25. Richard B. Gilbert, "Making the Spiritual Connection," *American Hospice Foundation Seminar Training Manual* (1998).

Chapter 7

26. Beverly Eanes, Lee Richmond, and Jean Link, *What Brings You to Life?* (Mahwah, NJ: Paulist Press, 2001), 2.

27. Macrina Wiederkehr, *Seasons of Your Heart: Prayers and Reflections* (New York: HarperCollins Publishers, 1991), 64.

Works Cited

Clairmont, Patsy et al. *Humor for a Woman's Heart.* West
Monroe, LA: Howard Publishing Co., 2001.

Eanes, Beverly, Lee Richmond, and Jean Link. *What Brings
You to Life?* Mahwah, NJ: Paulist Press, 2001.

Golden, Tom. "A Man's Grief." *M.E.N. Magazine*
(November 1994).

———. "A Tree for My Father." *M.E.N. Magazine* (March
1996).

Kagan, Henya. *Gili's Book.* New York: Teachers College
Press, 1998.

Klein, Allen. *The Healing Power of Humor.* Los Angeles:
Jeremy P. Tarcher, Inc., 1989.

Kübler-Ross, Elisabeth. *To Live Until We Say Goodbye.*
Englewood Cliffs, NJ: Prentice-Hall, Inc., 1978.

McConnell, Calvin D. Introduction, *Journeying Through*

the Days 1997. Nashville: The Upper Room, 1996.

McKissock, Dianne, and Mal McKissock. *Bereavement Counseling.* South Australia: Griffin Press, 1998.

Nouwen, Henri J.M. *In Memoriam.* Notre Dame, IN: Ave Maria Press, 1980.

Rando, Therese A. *Grieving: How to Go on Living When Someone You Love Dies.* Lexington, MA: Lexington Books, 1988.

Sunderland, Steve. "Funeral Director's Role at the Time of Loss." *American Funeral Director Newsletter* 9 (1992): 20.

Turner, Johanna. *Grief and Faith.* Washington: American Hospice Foundation, 1997.

Wiederkehr, Macrina. *Seasons of Your Heart: Prayers and Reflections.* New York: HarperCollins Publishers, 1991.

ILLUMINATIONBOOKS

Other Books in the Series

Everyday Virtues
    by John W. Crossin, OSFS

The Mysteries of Light
    by Roland J. Faley, TOR

Healing Mysteries
    by Adrian Gibbons Koester

Carrying the Cross with Christ
    by Joseph T. Sullivan

Saintly Deacons
    by Deacon Owen F. Cumming

Finding God Today
    by E. Springs Steele

Hail Mary and Rhythmic Breathing
    by Richard Galentino